Clothes in Colonial America

By Mark Thomas

Welcome
Books

Children's Press®
A Division of Scholastic Inc.
New York / Toronto / London / Auckland / Sydney
Mexico City / New Delhi / Hong Kong
Danbury, Connecticut

Photo Credits: Cover and p. 5 © IndexStock; pp. 7, 9, 11 © Rosen Publishing;
pp. 13, 15, 17, 19 © Colonial Williamsburg Foundation
Contributing Editor: Jennifer Silate
Book Design: Erica Clendening

Library of Congress Cataloging-in-Publication Data

Thomas, Mark, 1963–
Clothes in Colonial America / by Mark Thomas.
    p. cm. — (Colonial America)
    Includes index.
Summary: Simple text and photographs depict the clothes worn by people in Colonial America.
    ISBN 0-516-23932-5 (lib. bdg.) — ISBN 0-516-23490-0 (pbk.)
    1. Costume—United States—History—Juvenile literature. 2. United States—History—Colonial period,
ca. 1600–1775—Juvenile literature. [1. Costume—History. 2. United States—Social life and customs—
To 1775.] I. Title. II. Colonial America (Children's Press)

 GT607 T47 2002
 391'.00973'09032—dc21

                                                                          2001032340

Contents

People in **Colonial America** wore different clothes from what we wear today.

Men wore pants called **breeches**.

Breeches only went down to their knees.

In Colonial America, men also wore long coats.

They were called **frock coats**.

Many shoes had **buckles**.

11

Women wore long dresses.

The dresses had many **ruffles**.

13

Young boys and girls also wore dresses.

Their dresses were tied in the back.

15

Boys wore dresses until they were about seven years old.

Then they wore breeches.

Very young children wore special hats.

The hats were called pudding caps.

Pudding caps were padded to keep the children's heads safe.

19

Colonial Americans
wore many different kinds
of clothes.

21

New Words

breeches (**breech**-ihz) short pants worn
  by Colonial American men
buckles (**buhk**-uhlz) pieces of metal used
  to hold together the ends of a belt or strap
Colonial America (kuh-**loh**-nee-uhl uh-**mer**-uh-
  kuh) the time before the United States
  became a country (1620–1780)
frock coats (**frak kohts**) long coats
ruffles (**ruhf**-uhlz) wavy edges on shirts
  or dresses

To Find Out More

Books
Colonial Kids: An Activity Guide to Life in the New World
by Laurie Carlson
Chicago Review Press

Colonial Times from A to Z
by Bobbie Kalman
Crabtree Publishing

Web Site
Colonial Kids
http://library.thinkquest.org/J002611F/clothing.htm
Learn all about clothing in Colonial times on this Web site.

Index

About the Author

Mark Thomas has written more than fifty children's and young adult books. He writes and teaches in Florida.

Reading Consultants

Kris Flynn, Coordinator, Small School District Literacy, The San Diego County Office of Education

Shelly Forys, Certified Reading Recovery Specialist, W.J. Zahnow Elementary School, Waterloo, IL

Sue McAdams, Former President of the North Texas Reading Council of the IRA, and Early Literacy Consultant, Dallas, TX